30 Days on:

Growing through Grief

30 Days on:

Growing through Grief

a journal companion

Pr. sean lumsden

NoOffSwitichPress

Spokane, Washington

This book is available for bulk sales, promotions, premiums or fundraisers. Please contact the publisher at NoOffSwitch@Outlook.com for more information.

Abide in Me, and I in you. As the branch cannot bear fruit of itself unless it abides in the vine, so neither can you unless you abide in Me. I am the vine, you are the branches; he who abides in Me and I in him, he bears much fruit,

John 15.4

Contents

Introduction- Please Read

You hold in your hand both a journal companion and a reflection on a year of grieving.

In the previous, poorly-selling, '30 Days On _____' each day has a thought and a question to reflect upon in your journaling. Since this is a reflection on a year of grief and how to process grief, this booklet will not be as neat and orderly. Grief is never neat nor orderly.

So, in this booklet, some of the entries are short but most are longer. I have constructed a few questions roughly based on the length of each entry and wound up with over thirty questions. You're welcome.

I will state this later but please remember: Grief isn't only about physical death. Greif is about the helplessness we all feel in regards to making life 'work' on this planet. Grief over the death of a loved one is the worst, but grief over the death of dreams and relationships can be a very frequent visitor.

So enjoy...while this may sound like a heavy topic, please know that processing grief is how we grow into a healthier future.

From death...comes new life.

God Bless,

Pr sean

What I've learned this year

On December 27th of 2017 my lovely wife of twenty-five and a half years suddenly died. Three nights earlier on Christmas Eve, she started the flame that would light everyone's candles for our candle-light service. I told everyone "I am the most blessed man you've ever met" just before the closing prayer.

At 10:44 AM three days later, she was gone.

Lynne was a marathon runner; whose diet and exercise habits were the envy of everyone who knew her.

She had just finished a 5-mile run in 15-degree weather. Our family had made plans to get together for a day of lunch and bookstore shopping. One hour later, she was dead.

I've been a pastor for twenty-two years and have helped hundreds of people walk through the grief process. So now I ask myself...what have I learned?

The following is my top-ten list. The earlier points were things I learned purely from the experience of losing Lynne, while the later points were things I knew theoretically, but the grieving process gave me a new depth of knowledge.

Why am I sharing all this? My first response is I have no concept of personal boundaries... and Lynne would probably agree with that.

But a funny thing happened about seven months after she passed; I realized I was stronger than ever. Still grieving, still ugly-crying for no rational reason, still a recluse, still finding things funny that others would find morbid... but I was stronger for going through this process.

So please know...this is MY process. Maybe some of these thoughts help...maybe some don't. I fully understand this is far too short a booklet to fully talk through these issues. But it's a start. It's MY start.

While you may disagree with some of my conclusions, you can't disagree with my reality. I have walked through the valley of spouse death and now I fear no evil. Why? Because when Lynne died, I chose to bear the death of Jesus. I chose to seek the kingdom versus comfort. Paul writes in 2 Corinthians chapter 4, that when we bear the death of Jesus, more of the life of Jesus flows through us.

I sit here one year later, still sad, still mourning, but stronger because having the life of Jesus flow through you brings the two things we all are looking for: peace and joy.

My prayer is that as you read this, you can apply some of these thoughts to help you arrive in a similar place.

Day 1 : Reflect on times in your past where you've lost someone to death. What are the strongest thoughts associated with that time?

#10. Ugly crying has a mind of its own

On January 1st of 2018, my two sons and I were getting cabin fever. Lynne had been dead for three days and we didn't go out much. So, it was a holiday and we thought we needed to get OUT!

We chose to see the latest Star Wars movie. "Perfect!" I thought. This should get my mind off the sadness I am feeling for a couple of hours.

Arriving at the theater was the first blast of normalcy we had felt in a while. The night was cold, the line was long and the popcorn was hot.

The movie starts and I am immediately transported. Monsters are getting blown up, lasers are being shot and I am feeling like a kid again.

Then it hits me...I haven't cried for two hours.

I have spent the past three days crying about every twenty minutes. My crying sessions weren't that long but they were frequent. Each evening after Lynne died was spent watching Idina Menzel clips on YouTube and just ugly-crying with impunity. Accidently, I played Sting's song 'Why Should I Cry for You' which was written after his dad died. Not my smartest move. Even my youngest son chimed in: 'Dad! NO! I can't listen to this.'

Yeah...he was right.

So, about a half-hour into the movie I realize I haven't cried and that makes me sad. So, guess what I did… yep…I started ugly-crying in the theater. "Text me after the movie" was the last thing I told my boys as I bolted out at full-speed.

As I get into the hall I think 'whew, made it.' Wrong. My face and eyes must've been red and puffy because the looks people gave me normally would be reserved for someone coming out of 'Schindler's list.'

In fact, I swear I heard a woman say to her date: 'I can't imagine Star Wars would be so sad…'Her date replied, 'Star Wars nerds get upset over everything.'

So, after perplexing everyone walking towards me, I exit the theater and head into the mall. Finally, I'm safe. The mall is crowded but randomly crying middle-aged men isn't totally out of the ordinary at the Spokane Valley Mall. It is the Spokane Valley after all…

'Pull it together Lumsden!' screams my brain. So, I call a friend, go back to being charming-Sean for a few minutes and start to feel my emotional equilibrium being restored.

I see Macy's department store and I surmise looking at expensive clothes should force my brain into a tougher place. Approaching the watch section, I see some Movado watches. These have always been my favorites and trying some on would be a great fantasy to indulge in for a while.

The nice girl smiles as I approach the counter making me confident my tears have dried and I ask her if she has any new Movado's in stock. She smiles broadly and brings out a nice black version with bright blue hands.

"This one just came in… it retails for $650."

The new watch she hands me is the exact watch Lynne bought me (used of course) for Christmas two years ago.

Cue the ugly-crying.

Cue body-shaking, head-bobbing, lung-collapsing, cop-calling, mothers-taking-their-children-off-the streets ugly-crying.

A look came upon the clerk's face akin to getting the letter that you are being audited.

"Oh…no…um…don't be sad…they do go on sale sometimes…"

Poor girl.

I blubbered out 'thank you' and moved quickly towards the exit. Then, of course, grief-brain kicked in and I evaluated that turn of events as being the funniest thing EVER!!

So now I am ugly-crying and cackling with laughter simultaneously. Good times. Gooooood times.

I'll talk more about the nature of grief in the next entry, but for now understand that tears are your spirit interrupting your regularly scheduled thinking with a breaking message: I hurt.

Moving through the grief process will usually require a massive quantity of ugly crying. That's ok. Some people won't cry much or at all. That's ok as well.

Grief puts us face to face with our own mortality and powerlessness in this life. The hope while grieving is that the ripping, searing pain of grief can be shared with those we love and evolve into mourning. We all share in the love of the deceased, so we all share in the pain as we learn to reconcile our thoughts and feelings.

Remember: Grief is the price of love. Only those who love have the opportunity to grieve.

We used to live in a society that after a death, dressed in black for a year leading everyone in town to ask 'who died?' This simple moment allows the grieving person to share the story and thereby share in the mourning. Now we give you pills, tell you to pep-up and go on match.com.

Fortunately, I have learned that the only thing in this life you really control is your choice to step closer to Jesus or not. So, this booklet is my journey of consistently stepping closer.

Until then, ugly-crying is the reminder that you loved. There is some comfort in that even if the girl at the Macy counter never gets the whole story.

By the way... tears also may interrupt your regularly scheduled thinking to announce 'I can hope again. '

Day 2: When was the last time you cried? When was the last season you cried often? If you don't cry, how do you feel about that?

Day 3: How can tears be healing?

#9. Grief is a spider's web

Did you ever have someone in your life who had an opinion about EVERYTHING in your life?

Sean- when are you going to get a REAL JOB?

Sean- aren't 7 basses enough?

Sean- Visa is NOT meant to be your venture capitalist!

Grief is like that. Grief is a spider's web that has an opinion about every part of your life.

Sean- sarcasm is not a fruit of the spirit.

After Lynne's death I was overwhelmed with the immediate loss. Soon after, the implications of her death started to make themselves known.

All of this is very natural. You need to ask questions about your finances, home, child-raising and future.

The problem is, grief-brain is very real and very irrational.

Grief-brain is a combination of all your best thoughts and worst thoughts. All your thinking simultaneously stacked on top of one another, wrestling like twelve cats with their tails tied together.

Oh- and add on fatigue. Good Lord the fatigue.

You'll be neck-deep in sadness when fear will pop up out of nowhere. Then, as you address the fear, optimism will kick-down the door.

Optimism? Where have you been? Were you even invited? Then, pessimism will feel guilty that they were asleep on the job and chime in with 'were never gunna make it...we'll all be living in a box under a bridge...'

Sadly, the pessimistic, defeatist emotions will have home court advantage for a while. You will try to remain focused on celebrating your wife's life and the overwhelming faithfulness of God all while Debbie Downer is 'whaa-whaaing' in your ear talking about feline aids.

(If that made no sense to you...welcome to grief brain. I think its hysterical.)

The reason I call grief a spider's web is two-fold. First, like a spider's web, grief is nearly invisible. You'll be having a nice walk in the woods and then BAM you go face-first into a web while you try to spit anything out of your mouth all while being terrified SOMETHING got in your hair!

Someone quoted Monty Python right after Lynne's death and we laughed. Then I started ugly-crying because Holy Grail was the movie we watched right after we got engaged. Next, guilt hits me because I regrettably thought Holy Grail was a perfectly appropriate movie for post-engagement entertainment. Man, I was a nerd...

My other problem is when I feel the tears well up right behind my nose, the first word out of my mouth is rated 'R.' Which is quite convenient when it happens while I am preaching. 'Now kids, just 'cause Pastor Sean said a bad word doesn't mean you can.'

The other reason I call it a spider's web is the interconnectedness of grief. Men traditionally have waffle brains; everything in its category and n'er shall the categories meet. Women traditionally have spaghetti brains; every thought is connected to every other thought. Lynne and I used to call that a 'Lynne train-track jump.' She could go from talking about global warming to talking about the speed of concrete drying and never see any disconnection. I'd look at her funny and she would clarify; 'You know...because there are no worms on the dark side of the moon.'

My waffle brain needed Lynne's spaghetti brain and vice-versa. If we both had the same thoughts, we'd have the same blind spots. This is why we had an amazing marriage for most of our twenty-five years. We appreciated each other's perspectives and differences.

Grief similarly takes liberty with my usual water-tight logic. I've realized that part of the reason for this is guilt. When you are in a sad brain-space, guilt becomes a very loud voice. I had guilt over the tough eight years of marriage we were in before she passed. I had guilt over the things my boys lost out on because I lost a great deal of money. I had guilt for the many apologizes that stayed in my brain and never made it to Lynne's ears and heart.

Add all those things together and scotch seemed like the only logical conclusion. More on that later.

In the last entry, I mentioned how the only thing in life we really control is our choice to step closer to Jesus or not. As my heavy-heartedness threatened to become a permanent squatter in my life, I remembered one key thought: The loudest voice in my head is NEVER God.

As a Christian, I agree with Jesus that almost nothing that happens on this planet is God's will. God has all eternity to make things right for those who submit to Him. Until then, there is an active force of evil on this planet whose only job is to make people distrust the goodness of God. Once this distrust is in place, the devil can execute his plan to make people eternally miserable.

God's will and Satan's will are accomplished ONLY when people agree with them. I had to learn that even in my grief, I was making choices that were going to either insist on God's best or lazily allow this horrific loss to ruin life for myself and my sons.

How did I do that? I lived firmly placed in the thought that 'every thought in my brain is not me.' When I chose to turn up the volume on my thoughts that focused on the goodness of God and turned down the thoughts of anxiety, I was able to muddle through.

Was it easy? No. Scotch was easy, predictable, fast and controllable. But...more on that later.

Grief must be processed and reconciled. Don't EVER listen to someone that is talking about closure! The only closure is "I think you need to closure your mouth!" Closure doesn't happen but reconciliation with the reality can and does happen. For grief to become mourning we need to share our stories, thoughts and conflicts with people we feel safe around. That is where health and healing take place.

For me, I learned to separate the thoughts pointed to things I can't control from the thoughts that pointed to things I can control. In the process, I realized that some emotions just needed time to mellow out.

I learned to say, "this emotion will pass" and "it would be **nice** if I felt better, but it is **not necessary** for me to feel better right now."

And then I chose to step closer to Jesus as often as I could.

The great thing about spider webs... they demand to scare you. But you can walk right through them.

Day 4: Reflect on grief after a relationship problem. How is that similar or different than a grief after physical death?

Day 5: Reflect on another type of grief: how is that similar or different that a physical death?

Day 6: How does the thought "almost nothing on earth is God's will" sit with your thinking and experience?

#8. Anxiety is THE gateway drug

I live in Washington State. We were proudly the second state to make marijuana use legal. Yea us! That was sarcasm by the way...

Part of the argument against the legalization of weed was that weed was the 'gateway drug' that leads to harder drugs like heroin and meth. Once that argument was made, an opponent would say that alcohol is more of a gateway drug.

So, I started asking God 'what is the main gateway drug?' As I processed through my grief, I realized the main, if not only, gateway is anxiety.

Anxiety, in my mind, is the terror you feel in your body. Worry bounces around your brain like a puppy on steroids. Anxiety dwells in your body.

This was a personal issue for me since I have had seasons of wrestling with anxiety. Please note the word 'seasons.' My wife lived with anxiety her whole life and anxiety contributed to her far too early death.

When I was losing money hand over fist, I had my first panic attack. Every situation seemed to go backwards and I wanted to curl up in a ball and die. When I was audited by the IRS, my panic level was thermo-nuclear for about three months.

Lynne battled anxiety every day of her life. Running helped her body feel better when the anxiety threatened to immobilize her. Eating healthy was something she could control and helped her feel she had a sense of control in a world that never promises that benefit.

Unfortunately, eating healthy and exercising for Lynne was a dangerous combination. For most of her life, this combination empowered her to be an amazingly productive person and eventually become the greatest sign-language interpreter in the country. Sadly, elements of anorexia snuck into her thinking and she started eating less and exercising more. This combination wreaked havoc on her body.

She used to say, 'Anxiety is a lying bastard.' And yet, we all believe the core lie of anxiety which says, 'I am not enough to keep myself safe.' What you may have just noticed is that anxiety is really a way we process fear.

This feeling of real or perceived threats are what lead most of us to addictive behavior. When we come face-to-face with the reality that we can't make life 'work' for ourselves, we must self-medicate. Self-medication leads to self-sabotage which opens the door to self-destruction. If you've ever tried to love someone in self-destruction you know that people never self-destruct on their own. Eventually self-destruction becomes other-destruction.

Every suicide is really a suicide bomb. It doesn't matter if the person slowly kills themselves with alcohol or quickly with a gun; suicide spreads the pain from the person who dies to those who are still alive.

So how do we grow through anxiety? First, I have to disclaim that I am not a counselor, but I do help many people process these issues. Do not be afraid to find a good counselor to help you grow! They have helped me many times. If they recommend medication don't hesitate. What I am going to share is MY story. I hope it helps but if it doesn't, find YOUR story.

First, I have to discern the difference between discomfort and danger. In a grieving place (either from Lynne's death or general life grief) the two become very intertwined. As I processed that Lynne's health didn't get better it became too easy to look at every situation and think that nothing was going to get better...ever! I had to come to grips with the fact that every situation is in the middle of a war; but the more I fight for the right outcome, the more I'll win. I couldn't give up every fight just because one didn't turn out well.

I then had to appreciate that I may have survived trauma before while being anxious or depressed; my survival was not because of my anxiety or depression. My survival was IN SPITE OF these negative emotions.

The trick anxiety plays on us is believing that we survived in the past BECAUSE of the worry, fear and anxiety. This trick keeps us 'in debt' to the anxiety and not fighting against it. Our subconscious is thanking the very chains we are bound-up in! Imagine this, anxiety is like jail...you'll survive but you'll never thrive. I had to quickly realize that a better life existed for me outside of the anxiety trap.

The next thing I did was hijack my worry train. My brain got caught into many anxious circular-thinking traps. Each loop played out my excuses for failure and why my life fell apart after Lynne died. Health started when I began inserting thoughts of hope and faith into the worry. It sounded like this:

"After Lynne died, I became consumed with sadness that turned into lethargy. I started spending money recklessly and drinking excessively to numb the pain. **Then I turned my worry into worship and learned to thank God constantly and everything started turning around.'**

Now, who can tell which part was anxiety talking and which part was faith? I will stress, this was not easy nor intuitive. Scotch was both easy and intuitive. This took a level of grit I DID NOT HAVE...

In the natural.

Part of, if not all of discipleship is learning to live from your spirit and not your flesh. After Lynne's death, my flesh moved from a small part of my brain to front-and-center. I wanted 24/7 pity parties! But I realized I had to get back to living from my spirit QUICKLY!

So how did I learn to move back into living from my Spirit? Journaling Prayer, worship music and praying in my prayer language.

I'm not going to talk about my prayer language in this booklet, but I knew all the time I was praying in the Spirit I was praying God's highest good for every situation. The more time I spend praying in tongues releases more of God's prophetic voice into my mind. I pray mysteries to God, He releases prophetic insights to me.

Journaling prayer has been a mainstay in my faith for 27 years. To me, journaling is how we make our inner life visible. When we journal, we look at the thoughts, fears, phobias, hatreds as well as the faith and hope that is really kicking around. We are empowered to address the issues that don't agree with Jesus and turn up the volume on the thoughts that do agree! The first appendix section teaches journaling.

Finally, I spend exorbitant amounts of time listening to worship music. And when I say exorbitant, I mean an hour in the morning, 2 hours in the afternoon and 2 1/2 hours before I sleep.

Worship (in singing) brings the two sides of your brain together and takes the truth of God's word from your conscious brain into your subconscious. This is where deep healing happens. Anxiety and addictions are all in your subconscious. We all have fears that aren't rational; worship music helps get the word of God deeper than our brain to address some of our deepest issues.

So when the paramedics said 'time of death 10:44' my brain went to 'when I don't understand...I will choose you'...'You're a good good Father' or 'Because He Lives...I can face tomorrow' or 'if I never had a problem...I'd never know God could solve them, I'd never know what faith in His word could do...that's the reason I sing that through it all....'

When I received the worst news possible, my brain was ready to go to the truth of God's word because I have hid 40 years of God's word in my Spirit through worship music. If people tell me they have never heard the voice of God, I ask them if they have ever had a song pop up in the middle of a tough moment and they almost always answer that they have.

That is the voice of God! Would the devil want you singing 'How great is our God' during a traumatic event?

Other great ways to hijack your anxiety is to pretend that your anxious thoughts are a 'crazy uncle' who you can't shut up, but you can survive. Another great way is to imagine your worry is a horror movie you've already seen a few times. When the fear tries to kick in, you answer with 'OK, I've seen this before…everything is going to fall apart and I'll wind up living in a box under a bridge.'

You MUST change your relationship TO worry while you change your thoughts of WORRY. You can't out-shout your fears, but you can disempower their control over you.

So, in the process of losing Lynne I grew in my ability to process anxiety. I would encourage you to ask yourself what deep held fears are still kicking around in your soul. Asking these questions now will empower you when you go through your next crisis.

Day 8: How does your anxiety manifest itself?

Day 9: Do you have any healthy anxiety responses? Which ones would you like to develop?

Day 10: How is worship an element of your life? What are your favorite worship songs?

Day 11: If you were to allow your anxious thoughts to run, what would the central thoughts be? How would the Bible answer those thoughts?

#7. Joy feels like floating

Finish this sentence spoken by every modern parent:

"I just want my kids to be _____"

Or this one spoken by most divorcing people:

"I left my marriage because I just wasn't _____."

Happy.

If anxiety is the only gateway drug, happiness is the high we are all chasing.

Our nation is even founded on the premise that the benefit of freedom is the 'pursuit of happiness.'

Can I make one thing perfectly clear? The pursuit of happiness will ensure a life of never being happy or worse, the pursuit will leave you addicted to whatever gives you happiness.

Scotch promised me quick, predictable and manageable (at first) happiness. Fortunately, I knew that the price would have been addiction and most likely losing everything I held dear.

So, after my wife died, I did not pursue happiness; I pursued joy. Allow me to explain the difference.

Happiness is about what 'happens.' When everything lines up perfectly, our comfort zone is met perfectly, and we feel fleetingly 'happy.'

But as the great Theologian Don Draper said: "What is happiness? It's a moment before you need more happiness."

The problem with happiness is that once your comfort zone gets met, your comfort zone gets smaller. Next time, it will be harder to hit your comfort zone perfectly.

Have you ever met someone who was a 'foodie?' How hard is it to impress them with a dinner? Or ever met someone who only travels to the most exotic locales? How hard is it to keep them from getting bored? The reason so many wealthy people are hard to please is because their comfort zone has become microscopic.

It's not just rich people; in my 30 years of buying and selling over 40 bass guitars, I have very precise specifications for any bass I keep. And of course, since I am a Saab nerd, I turn my nose up at Porsches, Mercedes and any other car that will start every time. Cummon...they're Saabs... they're not supposed to start *every time...*

Joy is what Jesus promises to those who follow and agree with Him. **Joy is about your comfort zone progressively growing LARGER**. Joy says "I am comfortable anywhere the Comforter is."

The Comforter is the Holy Spirit and He lives in me and surrounds me. This means I am comfortable in every situation. Hmmm...didn't Paul say that:

Phil. 4. 11 I am not saying this because I am in need, for I have learned to be content whatever the circumstances. 12 I know what it is to be in need, and I know what it is to have plenty. I have learned the secret of being content in any and every situation, whether well fed or hungry, whether living in plenty or in want. 13 I can do all this through Him who gives me strength.

Note that the famous verse "I can do all things" is in direct reference to living with the vicissitudes and pressures of life. This, I believe, is Biblical joy: Being so convinced of Jesus' presence, power and purpose that nothing can shake you.

When I lost Lynne, the weight of sadness was crushing and ripping. There was no 'happiness' to be found.

But there was joy. Eventually.

After the first few weeks, when people would ask me how I was doing, I would say: "I am walking on water...the grief that should be consuming me is holding me up."

You have to understand...I am a preacher so I can't just say 'fine.'

This is where I learned that joy feels quite like floating. I know and acknowledge that I am surrounded by circumstances that could take me under. And yet... I am still buoyant.

Instead of pursuing 'happiness,' I pursued purpose. I asked myself 'how can I agree with Jesus today?' Somedays, it meant I didn't do much. Somedays, I was productive for a while, and just sat with my sons for a while. When I started back to work, I was as productive as I could be and didn't beat myself up if I wasn't feeling productive.

But I always stayed in prayer. Even if prayer was just reflecting on good times and tough times with Lynne by reading old journals.

I always stayed in worship. I would guess I was around worship music ten hours a day for the first month.

I read my Bible some and then a great deal. During the first month I only read the Psalms and Gospels. Please note, I said I READ the Bible, I didn't have it in me to STUDY the Bible. Then, 2 months after Lynne's death, I retired the Bible my then fiancée bought me 27 years ago on our first Christmas and bought a new one. With that new Bible in hand I read the entire New Testament each month, for a few months.

I wasn't able to study the Bible for a few months, but I knew my Spirit was being strengthened even if my mind was as sharp as a baked potato. I refused to allow grief to turn into addiction and staying close to Jesus ensured that outcome.

Here is what I learned in the process; Satan says pursue happiness and get bound to whatever makes you happy. Eventually that addiction will destroy you and everything you love. Jesus says pursue Me, and you will get liberated from everything and everybody. Eventually that pursuit will lead you into a life of impact where you will enhance the lives of everyone you love.

I'll talk more about living above anxiety later, but for now know that when our founding fathers wrote about the pursuit of happiness, the word 'happiness' meant a life of self-sacrifice for others. Jesus would call that...joy.

Day 12: Is there someone in your life or in your past that was addicted to being 'happy?' How did that play out?

Day 13: Reflect on the thought that Joy is increasing the size of your comfort zone. Where could your comfort zone grow?

Day 14: What Bible verses bring comfort to you when your comfort zone is being stretched?

#6A. Cry at God

The story of Jesus resurrecting Lazarus is very common, very powerful and very frequently misunderstood. In this story I believe we see how Jesus points us to handle our grief. If you open to John 11 you will notice immediately, the tension in this story is mesmerizing.

Lazarus, a friend of Jesus, is sick. Mary and Martha are also close with Jesus and dependent on their brother Lazarus.

The text says Lazarus is sick. Any reader would surmise that Jesus will heal his friend like He has healed everyone He encountered. Maybe Jesus will speak the word of healing or maybe He will send one of His disciples as he had done before.

This time...Jesus waits. Jesus waits until Lazarus is good and dead. When pressed by His disciples Jesus clearly says, 'Lazarus is dead.'

Hmmmmmm... we don't know how to file this.

When Jesus arrives, the funeral has been going for three days and the professional mourners are there.

Quick note, in America we don't grieve well. As I've said earlier, the hope in this whole process is that we move from personal grief to communal mourning. I learned during my time dealing with Lynne's death that very few people really stick with you during the whole process. In Israel during the time of Jesus, the communal aspect of mourning was firmly in place. Mary and Martha would not have been processing Lazarus' death alone.

But before Jesus can arrive at the home, Martha runs out to meet him bringing mankind's most common accusation against God:

"IF you had been here my brother wouldn't have died."

My mother wouldn't have gotten cancer!

My son wouldn't have overdosed on drugs!

My daughter wouldn't have died at 5!

I wouldn't have lost my job, my house and my marriage!

You've heard these cries before...you've probably raised these cries yourself. This is our first point:

Everyone on earth cries AT God.

Life guarantees two things: feeling powerless and death.

The reason every religion or philosophy has a form of prayer is because every human feels powerless on a regular basis. Granted, atheists don't have any form of prayer, but they have undoubtedly been furious at the forces of nature that bring about sickness and death. Maybe you could make the argument that their faith in scientists, doctors and medicine is their form of prayer.

This cry is echoed a verse or two later when Mary shows up and says the exact same thing:

"If you had been here my brother would not have died!"

I had a variation of that thought when the paramedic announced: 'time of death 10:44.'

'God!?!?! WHAT???' Pretty articulate huh...

There is a popular belief in American Christianity that its 'OK to be mad at God...He can take it!'

That is true; God can take our anger. The problem is we can't take being angry at God.

We can BE angry at God, but if we want to live healthily, we can't LIVE angry at God. Leaves can't live angry at the trunk that keeps them alive. I think at some point, God choses to wait your attitude out. He has time.

Please hear me clearly, if you are newly in grief do whatever you need to, think whatever you must to move forward into the next day. I know after Lynne's death, I went to bed pondering some thoughts that were not very pastor-like.

Just understand, your health is dependent on moving from anger at God to receiving from God. Which happens to be the next part of the story.

Day 15: When have you cried 'at' God?

Day 16: Who in your life is crying 'at' God right now?

#6B. Cry to God

As we move into the story we recap our first thought:

Everyone cries AT God.

We see though, that Martha didn't stop at crying in accusation at Jesus. She moves onto the next stage of health:

Some cry TO God.

She states: 'I know that God will give you whatever you ask.'

Martha quickly pivots from fear to faith. She acknowledges her powerlessness and Jesus' powerfulness.

Note Jesus' response; He does not say that death is 'God's will' or that this death was part of 'God's secret plan.' Instead He refocuses all of her attention on Him and His perspective on the spiritual battle.

I AM the resurrection and the life, anyone who believes in me will live even though they die and whoever live by me will never die- John 11.25

In the battle of life verses death and darkness verses light, Jesus and God are ALWAYS on the side of life and light. They are SO MUCH on the side of life that death is just a hallway to get to MORE LIFE!

Jesus then asks a very important question: 'do you believe this?' Remember, our response to and agreement with Jesus is the crux of Christianity and our life on earth. Anyplace you don't agree with Jesus is a place where He isn't your Lord and where you think you are smarter than Him.

Martha answers that she believes Jesus is the Son of God which sets up the next part of the story.

Before we get to that, lets recap this part of the story.

Everyone has faith. Even atheists have faith in scientists, the scientific process and the laws of nature. The question is who do you have faith in?

Martha cried TO God after she cried AT God. When grief rips you open, the quicker you can run back to Jesus the quicker He can heal the open wound.

Health happens when we learn to run TO God when everyone and everything tells us to run away FROM God. But remember; running from God always means running toward a lesser god. Sadly, these lesser gods usually require the price of addiction as their price of admission.

I was blessed to have thirty years of prayer preparation already active in my life when Lynne died. I knew what to do, how to do it and what to do when I had nothing in the emotional reserves. But more on that later...

There are no short-cuts to spiritual maturity. Ok... there might be one: Learn to make your best decisions on your worst days. Those moments when you choose to turn towards God when everything in your life is telling you to turn towards immediate satisfaction are transformative. These moments are like getting a 50% raise in your income and 50% cut in your expenses at the same time.

So Martha made a great choice...but we still have a third reality.

Day 17: What parts of prayer come easy to you? What parts are tougher?

Day 18: How has your prayer life changed over the years?

Day 19: How do you want your prayer life to improve?

#6C. Crying with God

Lets recap:

Everyone cries AT God

Some cry TO God

Martha had made her declaration of faith when Mary comes and accuses Jesus of not being there in time. Jesus sees Martha's faith and is ready to act.

Interestingly...Jesus makes an interesting request: 'Show me where you laid him.'

WHAT??? Jesus...are you deaf and blind??? We are in a fairly open area that is clearly lined with tombs, there is a group of wailing women just in front of You and You ask where Lazarus is buried??

People who have had more faith in their senses than in Jesus frequently thought Jesus was a little naïve. Remember when Jesus told the mourners that the little girl was 'not dead but merely sleeping?'

Spoiler alert: Jesus raised the dead girl.

Please note, Jesus is not asking a location question, He is asking a relationship question. Similar to when God asked Adam 'where are you?' God knew where Adam was hiding; He wanted Adam to reflect on their relationship.

Jesus wanted to know where Lazarus was laid so that Martha and Mary could reveal **where they gave up hope**.

So Jesus could cry with them.

Everyone cries AT God.

Some cry TO God.

Those who cry WITH God can see new life.

Where did you give up hope?

A hospital? A divorce court? A bankruptcy proceeding?

For me, it was my living room. Looking at my dead wife still dressed in her jogging clothes.

The path to healing begins with embracing our powerlessness in the presence of the all-powerful One. And crying together.

Why did Jesus cry? We serve a God that cries with us. We don't serve Allah who proclaims that everything good or evil is Allah's will. We don't follow Bhudda who tells us 'life is suffering' and we should meditate to disconnect from the illusion of connection and eventually eliminate desire. We don't serve Karma of Hinduism that would imply that Lynne's early death was a Karmic punishment for a past evil. We don't believe that this existence is just a product of time and chance and my pain is just a firing of synapses in my brain and my wife was no more than a bag of blood dancing to the beat of her DNA.

We serve a God who came into the suffering of this planet. Jesus allowed His creation to brutally murder Him. Then while being crucified, our God pled for His murderer's salvation so He could spend all eternity with those who murdered Him!

No human being would make up Christianity! Our hero was killed by his enemies and tells all His followers to do the same!

Joseph Campbell believes all religions tell the story of the 'Hero with a Thousand Masks.' The only difference is Jesus didn't defeat His earthly enemies; He allowed them to kill Him.

And that is where Christians must bring their thinking in line with Jesus'. Humans are not, and have never been the enemies of God. Satan is God's enemy. And at Jesus' resurrection Satan was defeated even though the war is still raging on.

For human beings to be judged by God, they must have irrevocable free will with full consequences. God will never override free will because at that point God ceases to be loving. God sovereignly gave humans free will and allowed them to kill Him with it. Yet even in Jesus' death, He was still sovereign. We killed Him and He didn't stay dead.

Our job now as Christians is to partner with Jesus to enforce the victory that was won at the cross and empty tomb.

And what did Jesus do after He wept with Mary and Martha? He brought Lazarus back from the dead.

In our case, we won't receive our loved ones back on this side of eternity. But Jesus can resurrect a new life with the memory of the loved ones. Mourning is the process of learning to go from living with the person, to living with their memory.

Don't let anyone tell you to gain 'closure.' There is no such thing. There is reconciliation. Reconciliation is coming to grips with our new life and the hope that exists for those of us 'in Christ.' That hope is that death is a promotion and we will be reunited with our loved ones soon.

Day 20: Write about the tension between crying with God and still fighting against the enemy.

Day 21: How do you learn to fight from your Spirit and not just your emotions?

#5. Survive vs. Thrive

So, this is going to be a tough entry. Why? Because of all my regrets, this is the issue I regret the most deeply.

Death brings regrets front and center. Everything I should've said and didn't. Every time I gave Lynne the cold-shoulder when she wanted to connect. Every time I should have dug deeper into our relationship but instead, I interpreted silence as peace and went back to being lazy.

Whew... this might be tough.

Fifteen-years before Lynne passed, I was fired by the church I helped start. This meant I had to find another career until a pastoring job opened. When people ask why I became a pastor I tell them 'because I have no marketable skills and an overwhelmingly huge need to be loved.' That doesn't fit well on a resume.

Eventually, I became a life insurance salesman and a financial planner. In the process I lost a large amount of money. That's right, I lost large amounts of money as a financial planner. Yes, the irony is ripe.

Fortunately, Lynne was making enough as a sign language interpreter to keep us afloat. Sadly, I had about two years where I didn't make any money and then we had some health issues that incurred health-care size bills. To be clear, our financial pit wasn't nearly as bad as it could have been, but for us it was overwhelming.

Eventually I started writing commercials, but I started at the bottom of the pay scale and had to work my way up. While I was making headway, the compounding interest on our debt was compounding at an alarming rate.

My next step was to go back to waiting tables at a local Italian restaurant. This was my version of Peter's going back to fishing after Jesus' death. I left Seattle when my oldest child was born so I could QUIT waiting tables. So, becoming a waiter again in my mid-thirties was about as humiliating an experience as I could envision.

This started a season of five years where Lynne and I became stuck in 'survival mode.' We've all probably had seasons like this. The pressing financial burden changed everything in our world.

Again, I want to stress that most people reading this have had far worse financial periods in their life, but for us this was a very real season of desperation.

The good news is we survived. Eventually I was asked to be the pastor of the church I am still pastoring. I was able to step back from the restaurant and focus only on pastoring and writing commercials.

The bad news is, Lynne and I were never able to get out of survival mode.

The worst news is, our boys never received all they could have from their parents. I never saw myself as a career driven man, but for those years I was driven to keep bills paid, debt lowered and the lights functioning.

For the six months while we prayed about becoming the pastors, our marriage was awesome. For the first six months after we were appointed pastors our marriage was even better. Lynne and I had the best year of marriage since our early years. And that is saying something.

After that blissful year, we went back into our old patterns of survival mode. Sadly, we never broke out. This led to three years of hating marriage and having eight toes out the door. This led to three years of marriage counseling. This led to three years of our sons hearing us fight.

And yes, I was a pastor during this entire time.

As I sit here almost ten years later, I can't point to any one thing that led to those horrific three years. We both danced a very dysfunctional dance we had been practicing for eighteen years. Neither of us handled our anxiety well, and when our partner didn't affirm us as we quietly demanded, we attacked.

That, ladies and gentlemen, is where getting stuck in survival mode will get you.

Survival mode is legitimate and better than non-survival mode (otherwise known as death.) Survival mode is when your brain detects danger and tells you to fight, take flight or freeze.

For those three years, Lynne and I both interpreted discomfort as danger. So, we fought instead of listening. We took flight instead of staying present. We froze instead of investing. It was hell on us, and even worse on our sons.

What should we have done? Instead of fighting for survival we should have invested in thriving. After three years of counseling we learned that we weren't in danger, but we were interpreting discomfort as danger. Our counselor helped us ask 'what is the threat?' and force our brains to discern what a gentle, healthy response would sound like. Eventually we found better, more grounded responses to tension.

Now, the good news is, two weeks before Lynne's death, we had a very nice lunch where we discussed long-term plans for the first time in eight years. We had survived the three years of hell and were making strides to patch up what was damaged.

Sadly, we never got back to good.

So, what is the point of this entry? The skills that ensured survival will sabotage any attempt at thriving.

When you are trying to survive, you accumulate to spend. Thriving takes a mentality of accumulating to invest.

Survival is a quick turn-around process. Thriving is about the long-haul. Survival is a credit card; Thriving is a mutual fund.

To survive you have to toughen up; to thrive you need to soften up.

Currently, I am trying to rebuild what was lost with my sons. I am intentionally trying to invest my time instead of spending it frivolously.

The bottom line is this: the loudest voice in your head is NEVER God. The enemy has been feeding lies into our brain for so long we think it is our own thinking.

Health happens when we learn to talk-back to our fears, worries and anxieties. Addiction's vocabulary is 'NOW, EASY, MORE.' Health's vocabulary is: I choose to wait and invest for God's best. If I sow healthy thinking and responding today, I will reap a harvest of health tomorrow.

Health happens when we let the thoughts of fear go through our brain and we don't respond like we did in the past.

Please note- you can't 'out-shout' your fears. With time, you can learn to 'turn-up' your healthy thinking.

The first step in going from survival mode to thrive-al mode is to treat your fearful thoughts as being annoying but not demanding. Your worry needs to be like an old uncle that goes on and on about the same things at every party. Or like your angry cousin that is obsessed with the latest conspiracy theory. You can't shut him up, you can only let him run himself out.

Another trick I use is to think of my worries as being a horror movie that I've seen repeatedly. I've seen 'Fatal Attraction' enough times that the fear is almost all gone. Every time I watch "The Shining" the cry of 'Red Rum' has less and less pull on my emotions. That is how you should approach anxiety.

And now, every time my fears try to tell me:

"Your wife died...you can't trust God."

"You have seen many people healed...but you failed to see your wife healed."

"Your stubbornness locked your wife in sadness the last year of her life."

I calmly let this goofy uncle go on and on and I quietly sing 'I stand in awe of You...and I'll let my words be few...Jesus I am so in love with You.'

Sometimes the fear passes quickly, sometimes it takes more time. But I NEVER let it have the last word and I NEVER allow it to trick me into believing that I am saying these things. And I NEVER take the self-sabotaging actions that promise instant numbness.

Remember, thoughts are not dangerous...actions are.

The voice of God is always calm, always encouraging and always telling me to get up and try again.

And THAT is the path towards thriving.

Day 22: When in your life was mere survival a pressing issue? What did you learn during that time?

Day 23: Did you develop any bad habits during this period?

Day 24: Have you ever switched from 'survival skills' to 'thriving skills?'

5B. Survive vs Thrive addendum

I must add this final point even though it doesn't coincide with the ten things I've learned.

When people met Lynne and me, they assumed I was always a pastor and Lynne was always an interpreter. And that assumption is close.

We came to Spokane so I could help start a church and Lynne could be a stay-at-home mom. When our oldest son was born, Lynne was having the time of her life staying at home and dreading having to go back to interpreting. Sadly, I was making almost nothing as a pastor and waiter, and we didn't have a choice.

When the offer came for us to go to Spokane we jumped at the chance. I could be a full-time pastor and Lynne could be a full-time mom.

Our world came crashing down when I was fired four years later. Even though there was no cause other than the Pastor's prerogative, this was still devastating.

In the swirl of 'what will we do' Lynne prayed 'Lord if you want me to interpret again, you'll have to bring it right to my door.' Allow me to clarify something... this isn't a smart thing to pray. God frequently tells us that we need to start knocking on doors. Nevertheless, God really loved Lynne and saw her heart.

Two days later a knock came on our door. Lynne opened the door up with our son on her hip and the woman asked, "are you the interpreter from Seattle??"

A week earlier, Lynne had told a woman that she was an interpreter during her aerobics class. That woman had a friend whose sister was deaf and needed a good interpreter.

Lynne worked a job or two with the woman and signed on with an interpreter agency in town. The next week Lynne booked a three-week job that paid her more than she ever made over the rest of her twenty-nine year career. In fact, that check was more than my three-month severance check. This knock on the door led Lynne into becoming the leading interpreter in the country for mental health issues among deaf people.

But that's not all…

During my time as a life insurance salesman, one of my first sales was to a woman I went to church with who ran a leading advertising agency in Spokane. She then realized I could sell effectively. After I failed as a life insurance salesman, I called her and begged her to give me a chance in the ad world. She took a chance and sixteen years later, I am still writing commercials with her.

My having an advertising career has enabled me to continue to pastor at a church that is in the poorest zip code in the state. My being bi-vocational helps our church pay small stipends to other people on our staff.

But that's not all...

Because I was in the life insurance industry after being fired, I purchased an acceptable sized policy on Lynne that kicked in upon her death. I am by no means rich, but I didn't have to panic after she died.

Are you noticing a pattern? Before Lynne's death, my being fired was the worst thing that happened to us. Yet, God took that and 'worked it together for good' just like Paul promised in Romans 8.28.

*And we know that God causes all things to work together for good to those who love God, **to those who are called according to His purpose.***

Now please note:

1. God doesn't cause all things. Jesus squarely points to Satan as the cause of 'killing, stealing and destroying' in John 10.10. God causes all things to **work together** for good. God's sovereignty is not about control but about resources. **All-powerful means all-resourceful NOT all-controlling**. Nothing can happen that God can't and won't work out for a believer's good.

2. This doesn't mean that the good that is 'worked together' will be better than the evil or pain that

occurred. It only means that evil will not have the last word. Nothing will replace the loss of my wife; but I am convinced God will bring good as He 'works together' circumstances.

3. God doesn't work things together for everyone on the planet nor for all people who are Christians. God does this for those who LOVE God. Those are people who spend time and talk to God. And those who are called according to HIS purpose. God's purpose is not Sean's purpose. BOTH conditions must be met. In other words, we must be disciples.

Lynne interpreted for hundreds of deaf people and trained thousands of interpreters.

I became a bi-vocational pastor and have the privilege to wash the feet of people who have injected heroin into those feet.

And all of this resulted from the worst thing that happened to us.

As of today, Lynne's death is the worst thing that ever happened to me. And yet, I get to share what I've learned with you so God has started working everything together for good.

Day 25: When have you seen God turn bad into good?

#4. Doing 'All Things' and Seeing 'Greater Things?'

After Lynne died, I was amazed to piece together how many ways God prepared me in the months leading up to her passing. This entry is a reflection on the reoccurring themes in the months prior to her death.

The first six weeks as a widower were a blur. My mental space was focused mainly on taking care of my sons and then myself. After about a month I started preaching and writing commercials again.

As my thoughts swirled and my emotions carbonated, I kept asking myself 'how do I move forward?' Everything seemed overwhelming and everybody was loving but I wasn't ready to tell everyone everything that they wanted to hear.

"I can't do this!' was simultaneously a voice and its own echo playing on an infinite loop in my brain. Fortunately, I have learned that 'I can do all things through Christ who gives me strength (Phil. 4.13).'

As a younger man, that verse was a challenge to dream big, to set impossible goals and watch God empower you towards changing your world.

As an older widower I think I learned more of what Paul meant when he wrote that. If you read the context of the passage, you receive a clearer picture of what led to this conclusion:

4.11 I have learned to be content whatever the circumstances. 12 I know what it is to be in need, and I know what it is to have plenty. I have learned the secret of being content in any and every situation, whether well fed or hungry, whether living in plenty or in want. 13 I can do all this through him who gives me strength.

Paul isn't telling people to dream big as much as he is telling them that they can persevere through anything. Doing 'all things' is really a statement of peace in the storm, more than conquering the mountain.

During this time, I learned that Christianity doesn't make life easy...it makes Christians strong. As we learn to agree with Jesus and make better choices, we stop sabotaging ourselves, which can make life easier.

I couldn't bring Lynne back or undo hundreds of lazy choices, but I could lean into the reality that God was still with me and I could come out of this grief stronger than ever.

What would 'stronger than ever' look like? As I pondered this question, I kept coming back to one of the greatest promises of Jesus: those who believe in Him will do greater things than He did (John 14.2).

Please note; that is not TBN...that is Jesus. The promise He gave on his last message before the cross was that His work would increase based on the obedience of His disciples.

I was at a point in my life where I was just foolish enough to believe Him. I started to realign my Spirit to believe that 'greater things' were part of the 'all things' that were potential to Christians.

But how do we get there? As I meditated on this proposal, I remembered there was another instance that sounded familiar to 'all things' and 'greater things'... it was 'all these things' and the speaker was Jesus Himself.

Matt. 6.33 But seek ye first the kingdom of God, and his righteousness; and all these things shall be added unto you.

There it was; I can do all things, including greater things if I seek first the Kingdom.

Now a quick note; The Kingdom of God is not the kingdom of Sean nor the comfort of Sean.

And His righteousness is God's highest good in any situation. Not my highest comfort, convenience or celebration.

But I had a way forward! My grieving brain, with anxieties bouncing off one another, could settle down long enough to have one goal for the day: Seek First.

Interesting timing, but right after this thought became solidified, I found out how Jesus grieved.

Jesus had just heard that John the Baptist was killed. We believe John and Jesus were cousins and probably grew up in some proximity together.

Matthew records in chapter fourteen, when Jesus heard about John the Baptist's death, He wanted to get away. I got that. When Lynne died, I withdrew to be with my boys as my main priority.

Yet, the text says the crowd followed Him. I would have told the crowds to leave me alone with great enthusiasm. What was Jesus' response? He was moved with compassion and healed the sick in the crowd. Since the crowd was large, the disciples came to Jesus to talk about dinner. I always love the disciples being interested in eating... sounds like my church.

Jesus, being tired and grieving, was ready to do more delegating; 'You feed them!'

The disciples heard this and did what most disciples are good at doing; they told Jesus why His plan wouldn't work. In this case they didn't have enough food. They knew exactly how much they did have: five loaves of bread and three small fish. They had a firm grasp on their faith in their counting ability.

'Bring them to Me.' A grieving Jesus still believed in God's power to move mightily. After Jesus gave thanks, He broke the bread and fish. Please note, before thanks and brokenness, the number of loaves and fish were fixed. But after the resources were given to Jesus, given thanks to God for, and broken, the number went from finite to infinite. Not enough to more than enough. Scarce to abundant.

Grief is the ultimate brokenness on this planet. Yet, in God's hands, your brokenness can and will expand your ability to impact those around you.

You may wonder how you can be thankful while grieving. Please remember, the Bible doesn't say to be thankful FOR all things just be thankful IN THE MIDST of all things (1 Thess. 5.18). I was never thankful for my wife's death. I was thankful for the goodness of God regardless of my circumstances. When your circumstances can't shake your thankfulness, you become undefeatable.

Jesus continues to seek solitude, so He dismisses the crowd. Finally, Jesus is alone and is able to pray. But while He is praying, He sees the disciples on a boat being tossed about in a storm.

Jesus then does what any of us would... He decides to walk on the water. As He approaches the boat, the disciples freak out because they think that Jesus coming to rescue them, is a harmful ghost.

Death can be discerned as being a harmful force if you are not grounded in the goodness of God. In fact, **your life will never be settled until the goodness of God is settled.** When you are convinced that your security and significance are in Jesus and Jesus alone, you will be able to remain in peace while all of the disciples around you are freaking out at God's absence. Your peace becomes YOUR proof of God's presence.

Only Peter has faith that Jesus can work the miraculous for them like He just worked the miraculous for the hungry crowd. So, he asks an important question; "Lord, is it you?"

Its ok to ask Jesus for conformation before jumping out of the boat. Just make sure you are set in your spirit to get out if He asks you to get out.

Peter steps out of the boat and experiences a level of the supernatural power of God that no one else has ever experienced. The other disciples remained terrified that 'God's SOVVVVV-ERIGN will has left them in a boat to die...God is allowing the devil to drown us...God's secret plan must be teaching us a lesson by leaving us in a storm.' How many churches are full of people who think the power of Jesus is really a harmful ghost?

As long as Peter kept his eyes on Jesus, the very waves that threatened to pull him under, kept him afloat.

That is what joy feels like. When people asked me how I was doing after Lynne's death, I told them I was 'walking on water.' The forces that were threatening to kill me were actually supporting me.

But the biggest miracle is yet to come.

The end of Matthew 14 is Jesus landing at Gennesarat. As usual the people of the city heard of His landing and brought their sick out to be healed. But if you look very closely, there is a difference; Jesus doesn't lay His hands on them, they lay THEIR hands on Him.

Get the size of this; Jesus had so much life and healing flowing from Him, that people were healed just because THEY touched HIM. These healings were not God reaching out to people...they were people reaching out to God.

How awesome will it be when Sunday morning church is people who are sick coming into church and walking up to any Christian, touching them and being healed?

THAT would repair America's health care problem very quickly.

Jesus healed a crowd. Jesus fed the 4,000. Jesus walked on water. Sick people were healed by touching Jesus.

All while Jesus was grieving the death of His best friend.

You may not like this conclusion...but you can't argue the Biblical timeline.

On Jesus' worst day He still chose to 'seek first' the Kingdom. And He did some 'great things' and challenges us to do 'even greater things.'

Day 26: What does 'seeking first' look like in your context?

Day 27: What are the biggest hindrances to your living 'seek first?'

Day 28: How does Jesus' activities while grieving say to you?

#3. Learn to Pray Before the Crisis

This entry was the first thing I learned after my wife's death; I am glad I knew how to pray before I hit this crisis.

As a pastor, I hear about a new crisis in someone's life almost daily. They ask me to pray and I gladly do.

But...

Frequently, I fear that the person I am praying for doesn't know how to intercede for themselves. Please get this: Your pastor cannot pray for you as powerfully as you can pray for yourself! All I can do as a pastor (or all anyone can do praying for another person), is bless the praying that they are doing themselves.

I'm sorry if that scares you, but part of the strength that comes from prayer is you using your willpower to choose the power of God's will.

From the fall of man until today, the fight for humanity is a fight over willpower. God knows as people use their willpower to choose God's will, they get set free as individuals and everyone around them is blessed in the process. Prayer is not just about 'getting answers;' it's about getting ourselves out of God's way so He can bless us and everyone around us.

Sadly, in America we see prayer as a pop machine; I put in requests and God gives me what I want. Prayer is closer to a power strip. I submit my will (the power strip) by plugging into God's will (the outlet) and His life and will flow through me into the situation and person I am praying for. If you don't have the discipline to stay plugged into God through prayer and obedience, you won't have much of God's power flowing into your situations. Jesus abided fully into the life of the Father and when He prayed, God's life flowed unhindered into those He prayed for. Our job is to use our prayer time to choose God's highest will over our most comfortable want.

If this is new for you, please pick up my booklet: 30 Days on Praying Like Jesus and 30 Days on Practical Impact.

Remember; nothing changes until your prayer life changes.

Fortunately for me, I learned how to pray as a teenager. My youth pastor, Greg, taught us to pray for an hour a day. I haven't always done that, but at this point in my life sitting in one place and praying for an hour is very easy.

The morning after Lynne passed, I knew my future, my son's futures and the future of the church I lead hinged on my response. The devil loves to swoop in during crisis moments and sow seeds of doubt towards God that can derail a person's life of faith for decades. I felt that potential like a scarf being wrapped too tightly.

The difficult part was my brain was fogged-in like a steam room. I felt nothing but sadness. I couldn't muster up any thoughts of faith. Feelings of anxiety swarmed in like flies. I had slept a grand total of zero minutes the night before and here it was 4:30 AM and I was wide awake and ugly crying like my life depends on it.

And I knew I had to pray.

So, I picked up my prayer journal and wrote, 'Ok God...here I am. You are good, You are faithful and You will never change.' That was all I had inside of me.

I put on some worship music and just listened. And then I grabbed some old journals and started reading all the amazing things God had done for me and my family.

Eventually I stumbled onto the part of my journal called 'God's Hall of Fame' where I have listed all the undisputable miracles I've encountered.

Next, I came upon the part of my journal called 'God's All-Star Game.' This is a list of near-miracles that I want to remember. Others may not call them miracles, but I don't care; this is my journal.

After that, I came to my declarations of agreement that state who I am in Jesus. Everything in my brain was screaming;

Loser, Widower, Bad Husband, Bad Father, Single-income provider, You'll lose the house, You can't put your sons through college, you'll never retire, You'll be broke!

And the list told me:

I am who Jesus says I am.

I am blessed in the city, in the field, when I arrive and when I depart.

Finally, I came upon my list of names whom intercede for. Lynne's name was first on the list...so that started me ugly-crying again. But then I saw Zach (my oldest) and Alex (my youngest) and the 300 or so people that were still in my life. I might have only said 'Lord, bless them' as I passed by their name, but I passed by their names.

Then I sat and prayed in my prayer language while listening to worship music for a couple of hours.

Did I then get up and rejoice? No. Did I arise and conquer? No. Did I still want to crawl into a scotch bottle? A little.

What happened? I refused to be a victim of my own negative thinking. I chose to agree with Jesus and not my own potentially destructive thoughts.

I still grieved...but I wasn't a victim of grief. I didn't feel like myself for about six months. And even then, that was a hit or miss feeling.

Most importantly, I didn't bow down to my feelings if they didn't bow down to Jesus.

Here is the point: I was able to bear in my body the death of Jesus so that more life from Jesus could flow out of my body. No weapon- even the death of my beloved wife of 25 years- was going to prosper. It may hack out a pound of flesh or two...or three...or twelve. But the weapon of powerlessness was NOT going to ever make me a victim of my own negative thinking.

But, I had to learn how to pray THROUGH the crisis before I entered the crisis.

I sit here today, fourteen months after Lynne's death and my prayer-life is stronger than ever. My emotions are healthier than ever. My joy is greater than ever. I still have huge hours of sadness at missing my bride. But please note I said hours and not days.

The other reality I have to attribute my surviving the death of Lynne is that I taught my church how to pray. They have been lifting me up nonstop since the day they heard of Lynne's death. I learned how to pray before the crisis, and I taught them how to pray-us-through a crisis before the crisis.

So how did I not get bitter towards God? Those are the last two points.

Day 29: If you received horrible news today, how ready are you to intercede until you get the breakthrough?

#2.Goodness of God vs Cursedness of the planet

I learned this concept long before Lynne died. But after her death, I experienced this concept more deeply than ever before.

When I began preaching again, I noted that the last series I completed was called 'Pastoring your Shipwreck.'

At Living Hope, our driving Biblical story was about Paul's shipwreck. In this story, Paul makes his way to Rome and on the way encounters a shipwreck. Paul pastors all the people on the boat bringing them safely to shore. Then after he is bitten by a snake, he shakes off the danger and heals an entire city. All while getting to his destiny: Rome.

The main thought of this story is that every believer has a destiny like Paul's destiny was Rome. We are to expect shipwrecks, snakes and troubles on the way. God's promise on our life is about us getting to Rome...not the boat. We obsess about losing boats while God is focused on getting us to Rome.

I couldn't pick up telling this story after Lynne's death because I had a hard time believing that my marriage was shipwrecked on my path to Rome. That was tough. But that wasn't the final word... more on that later.

But first, let's clarify a few thoughts: Christians like to say the planet is 'fallen.' That is close. This planet right now is cursed. If you read God's reaction to Adam and Eve giving their authority to the serpent, you will see that God cursed this planet.

Let me clarify, cursedness and blessedness are paths, not moments. The moment mankind fell, we started on a path of cursedness. Adam and Eve did not die immediately but they started down the path of death. Sadly, their child was the first to die. Selah.

This planet, according to the Bible, is a demon-inhabited, disease-infested, waiting room between heaven and hell. It's also God's footstool and full of His glory. Beauty and horror simultaneously.

Earth is a war zone. God's will is only done by people agreeing with Him. When we say God is all-powerful, we mean: **All-powerful means All-resourceful not All-controlling.** No matter what horrible thing happens to you, God has a plan and the power to redeem that situation for good AS LONG AS YOU AGREE AND COOPERATE WIH HIM.

Look at the cross; Jesus willingly obeyed the Father into the worst death humans could imagine. Not only did that choice result in the resurrection, but our salvation came out of that horrific situation as well.

You have undoubtedly heard people ask 'why would God do this?' Or, 'why would God allow this to happen?' Its very simple; God doesn't micro-manage the planet. Satan is the warlord of this planet until Jesus returns. Both God and Satan are looking for people to agree with them in order to get their will done. God doesn't 'allow' suffering any more than a cop allows a robbery. God didn't allow evil; Adam did.

God is Love (1 John 4.8). Love demands free will like a banana needs a peel. Love is the result of free will. You can't put a gun to someone's head and say 'LOVE ME.' Also, free will requires predictable consequences for a person's choice to have influence in the world. Human choices are the deciding force for eternity. If God ever over-rode someone's free will He would cease to be loving.

Conversely, Satan is always trying to override your free will through addiction. Jesus simply says: 'follow Me.'

Jesus never, NEVER blamed God for sin, sickness, evil or death. In fact, He overthrew death and sickness everywhere He went, saying 'this is what the Kingdom looks like.'

Let's get this straight; planes flying into the World Trade Center is NOT God's will. Men and women bravely running toward those buildings IS God's will.

I find it ironic that people call a natural disaster an 'act of God.' Jesus explicitly says the thief (Satan) comes to steal, kill and destroy and Jesus comes to give abundant life (John 10.10). When you see nature killing and destroying, you can rest assured the reason for this destruction is because the 'whole planet groans waiting for the sons of God to be revealed (Rom 8. 22).' The planet is a mess because believers haven't risen to their full status as Kingdom enforcers. So the next time you hear the phrase 'act of God' you can look for the rescuers and volunteers running toward the problem...they are the ones doing an 'act of God.'

The other problem is some Christians believe everything is 'God's will.' Please note, if you want God to micro-manage the universe, then Islam is the faith for you. Jesus came to 'destroy the works of the devil (1 John 3.8) and to 'deliver us from the dominion of darkness (Col 1.13).' God does not play both sides of the chess board.

God's will is done by believers who BOTH 'pray-in' His will and 'obey-in' His will. We intercede and interact. Our job as Jesus followers is to find places where God's will is NOT being done and step in like the Kingdom police force that we are.

Remember, when we come into a situation where it looks like the enemy is winning, it is because he has already sown AND reaped darkness. Our job is to start sowing light until the light overcomes the darkness. Jesus lived in such agreement that He released more light with a word than most Christians do in a lifetime.

As we grow in agreement of thought, alignment of action and intimacy in emotions, we can become the light of the world as Jesus promised we would be.

Until then we learn to love the fight. You may be exhausted by spiritual warfare but know your spirit loves the fight and loves seeing your world become His world.

When the paramedics said 'time of death: 10:44' I came face to face with the cursedness of the planet.

I have seen hundreds of people immediately healed physically and thousands healed progressively through prayer.

And yet... the person I had prayed for the most in my life was lying dead in my living room.

Why?

From where I sit today, I have a couple of answers. Please note, answers don't bring comfort...just more questions. Only Jesus brings comfort. Nevertheless, I do have a few thoughts.

First, God may have been protecting her from a long, protracted illness. When she suffered a brain bleed five years earlier, I sensed God ask me "If I took her now, could you trust that I am protecting her from something worse?" I of course, questioned God's theology, but then acquiesced that yes, I could trust Him. I was watching my best friend walk his mom through her fourth year of Alzheimer's and knew that was hell on all involved.

The moment I said 'Yes, I'll trust you' my panic and fear left, and I walked out the next six weeks of her healing in peace.

Secondly, there may not have been anyone around that could get her completely healed. I know some of you are balking that 'God can do anything!' Yes, God can do anything. He chose to work through people though. Let me explain.

When I go to pray for someone, I tell them that if Jesus were standing here, they would be instantly healed. Sadly, they are stuck with me. Every time I pray for someone, I pull them back further from the waterfall of physical death. Jesus pulled people miles back from the waterfall. I may only pull them back a few blocks. This is why we gang up in prayer with other believers, to increase the power we are releasing from the rivers of living water in us.

Lynne's hidden physical issues may have progressed to a point where Jesus mercifully took her home. She had just taught hundreds of interpreters and received a very prestigious award acknowledging her contributions to the field. She may have finished her race.

This has not changed my thinking on healing one bit. I still contend that Jesus still heals and every time we pray, we add to the praying that has gone before. This is a battle in which believers must engage.

Until then, I don't see Lynne's death as either a victory or a defeat.

I see her passing as a stalemate.

She's in a better place and I am getting to a better place. Her death answered a question to those around her that felt there was 'something' wrong. Bottom line, God is still good, and this life is not all there is.

So how did I reconcile my path to Rome with my marriage seemingly being shipwrecked? Easy... it wasn't about me.

Lynne arrived at her Rome.

And I can live with that because this life isn't all there is.

Day 30: What is easier for you to embrace, the goodness of God or the cursedness of the planet?

Day 31: How does your understanding of healing work with the idea of the 'waterfall called death?'

Day 32: What is your 'Rome?' What do you think your destiny is about?

1. I'm still….

The number one thing I've learned since my wife died is: I am still the most blessed man you've ever met.

When I said goodnight to the people from my church on Christmas Eve before Lynne died, I looked out on a sea of candles and a packed sanctuary filled with all the people I love.

I knew this was the last Christmas before my youngest went off to college, so I was a little more wistful than usual. Our family tradition was to get take-out Thai food and open gifts.

With a full heart, I bid everyone Merry Christmas by telling them that I loved them and that I was the most blessed man they know.

Sadly, that thought was deeply shaken when Lynne was dead thirty-nine hours later. Almost twenty-six years of marriage over with the statement: 'Time of death, 10:44.'

I was just crazy enough to believe God's word.

2 Cor 4.7 *But we have this treasure in earthen vessels, so that the surpassing greatness of the power will be of God and not from ourselves; we are afflicted in every way, but not crushed; perplexed, but not despairing; persecuted, but not forsaken; struck down, but not destroyed;* **always carrying about in the body the dying of Jesus, so that the life of Jesus also may be manifested in our body.** *11 For we*

*who live are constantly being delivered over to death for Jesus' sake, **so that the life of Jesus also may be manifested in our mortal flesh**.... knowing that He who raised the Lord Jesus **will raise us also with Jesus and will present us with you.***

*16 **Therefore we do not lose heart, but though our outer man is decaying, yet our inner man is being renewed day by day.** For momentary, light affliction is producing for us an eternal weight of glory far beyond all comparison, while we look not at the things which are seen, but at the things which are not seen; **for the things which are seen are temporal, but the things which are not seen are eternal.***

I've mentioned before that the first verse in bold was my scriptural obsession in the three months before Lynne's death. I quickly meditated on how if I lean into Jesus, more of His life will impact my world because of the trauma I was living through currently.

The second highlighted thoughts were the ones that became very real to me. Heaven and eternity are real. Why do I believe that? Because Jesus did. Jesus believed so much in heaven and hell that He chose the cross over being rescued by angles.

Eternity is in the balance when human free will and predictable consequences are discussed. The reason free will cannot be violated is because God is Love. Love requires freedom like an apple requires a tree. The reason free will consequences must play-out in a predictable fashion is because God is just. He will act to maximize good and minimize evil, but humans need to see the consequences of their choices.

God will not have any human say He sent them to hell. Our choices determine our eternal destiny. If you've spent your life telling God to leave you alone, He eventually will.

Remember, Hell is a loving God giving people what they love most...independence from Him.

I also believe in life after death because we've all died before. It is called child-birth. When we were born into the world, our 'womb life' died. When you were in the womb, you could hear, feel and think. No matter how much your mom and dad spoke to you before birth, you could not fathom what came after. Our birth was our first death.

The same is true with this life.

I will see my wife again. She made it to heaven, and undoubtedly was met by her father and grandmother. Knowing her dad, he had a bike ready for the two of them to go for a ride. Knowing her grandmother, she had a scrabble board set up and the Scrabble Dictionary (her families other Bible) to make sure she didn't cheat!

This life is a blip. Eternity is where Jesus gets to repay all of those people who chose to believe in the eternal realities while the temporal realities screamed for our attention.

I choose to invest in people. I choose to invest in prayer. I choose to self-sacrifice like Jesus did.

Why? Because if Easter teaches us one thing it's this: self-sacrificial love is stronger than death.

Jesus rose again and on the Day of Pentecost, the same power that arose Him came to dwell in humanity. And that power gives me the faith to know that I will see my beloved wife again.

And because He lives... I can face tomorrow.

Because He lives...all fear is gone.

Because I know...I KNOW who holds the future.

And life is worth the living...Just because He lives.

I am the most blessed man you've ever met. Why? Because I am blessed even when it doesn't look like I'm blessed.

The goodness of God, the love of Jesus and the power of the Spirit all fill me with the hope of eternity.

And THAT is more powerful than death.

Day 33: When has God brought blessing from a situation that didn't look like God was blessing you?

Day 34: Where have patches of flesh been ripped out of you? How much faith do you have that more of Jesus is being seen?

Day 35: If eternity is real...how should your thinking change?

Day 36: How can you remember to think of eternity during the difficulties of life?

Appendix 1

Why Journal?

If you've never journaled, allow me to invite you into one of the greatest activities a person can get involved with.

Journaling is a spiritual discipline where each person takes their walk with Jesus seriously enough to create a tangible record. Now don't get intimidated...journaling is as easy or as complex as you wish to make it. Journaling can be as easy as writing down a thought you read in scripture, a prayer request and something you are thankful for.

Journaling can be as complex as working through deeply held beliefs and struggles under the umbrella of prayer. Your call. Remember, journal as you can... not as you can't.

A great starting place would be:

- Start with being thankful for a few specific things.
- Ask God to bring His will into specific situations on your heart.
- Ask God to fulfill any needs you may have.

If you have some issues in your character that may need God's touch, be sure to write those down to chart how far you have come.

Next, move to writing down a thought or two from your Bible reading that day. This booklet is designed to jump start your writing with stimulating subjects. If all else fails, open up to the Psalms (usually right in the middle) and read until you find a verse that echoes your thoughts for the day. You can be specific or general in your writing. You can even use codes if you fear someone reading them. Remember, you set the rules.

Now, if you really want to grow, be sure to tell people the good news you find. The fastest way to grow is to make a habit of telling people what you are learning on a daily basis. When I find something good, I try to tell five people that day. In Christianity, you only keep what you give away.

The most exciting part is when you look back and see how God has answered prayer, changed your character or seen how He has spoken to you while you were processing your thoughts.

Good luck and God bless!

Appendix 2 Prayer tips

Prayer list:

I strongly recommend creating a prayer list of people and situations in your journal. You don't have to follow the list, but if you are anything like me, you have had times where you sat down to pray and your mind goes blank. This is why a list helps.

You don't have to feel tied to the list, but this will help you keep moving forward in prayer on those times your brain is not fully engaged. Your spirit is always engaged...your brain...not-so-much. You can actually write down prayers for each person on your list, or just use the names to remind you to mention them in prayer.

Prayer times:

Jesus prayed both early and late. I'm guessing through the day as well. Currently with my wacky schedule I have six times during my day where I can fit in 15-20 minutes in prayer. If I make three of those times in a day I feel pretty good. I try to make sure that I spend at least one of those times in my prayer language and one of those times journaling.

Those are my set times; I also try to steal times. Stolen times are when you are praying while doing something else. Time in the shower or car are great opportunities. But remember... my stolen times are better when I am making my set times. If all you are trying to do is steal time or pray on the run, I fear you may not have made prayer a real priority. We come to God for salvation on His terms. We should avoid coming to Him in prayer on our terms.

Praying in your mind as the day goes on is closer to meditation than intercession. Meditation is a good practice and certainly better than using your mind to rehearse old grievances or the state of the Mariner's bullpen. But...I don't think all of heaven jumps to attention when you worry and occasionally say God. Bill Johnson famously says, "If your prayer doesn't move you, why do you think it will move God?"

I believe intercession starts when your world stops. If you had waited six months to get in with a brain surgeon, would you have your phone on, Grey's Anatomy on, your lap top open and be plucking your eyebrows during the meeting?

Meditation:

Meditation is God-focused thinking. Eastern meditation is about emptying yourself to join with a cosmic one-ness. Christian meditation is focusing your mind on the truth of God to allow His word to take root in your spirit. Silent prayer would or should fall in this category. When we meditate, we give God the reigns to our mind and we make mental / spiritual connections to the truths we are focusing on.

I will take a verse, story or song and just chew on it all day and watch what God brings to the surface. Eighty-five percent of what I preach on any given Sunday has come from my meditation time. This is also where most of my analogies come from. Last night while I was meditating on my dog walk, my dog bolted away because she smelled something. Meditation is like that...you will start meditating on a subject, and God will drop a thought into your brain and you will mentally pursue the thought like my dog did the smell. This is a huge way to integrate the truth of God's word into the day-to-day of life. What you focus your mind on you empower. If you focus on worry you empower fear. If you focus on God's truth, you empower Him. One brings anxiety...the other brings peace.

Hearing God's Voice:

The first and easiest way for God to speak to you is through worship music. When a song comes into your brain GRAB IT! This is the voice of God!

If you wish to grow in this gift, take apart that song as a meditation exercise. For example, if "Jesus Messiah" comes to mind, I will think: 'He became sin who knew no sin... what sins of mine did He take to the cross? Am I getting free from them?'

'Name above all names... One of God's names is Jehovah-Jireh: God will provide. The word says that at the feet of Jesus every knee will bow... so I speak to my fear of poverty and command it to bow its knee at the feet of Jesus.'

See how I took the thoughts of the song and made them real in my life? If you show God you are serious about hearing His voice He will speak more.

The last thought about hearing God's voice this is the more scripture you have in your brain, the more God will bring to your attention and the more you will discern how precise you are in hearing His voice. Without a doubt or qualification, the most prophetic people I have ever known are the people who know the Word the best. God will NEVER contradict His revealed word with a prophetic word.

So, find a verse, or worship song and let it take over your mind for a day!

Appendix 3

Statements of Agreement

After Lynne died, I made sure I read my statement of agreements at least once a day. Remember, these statements are true whether you agree or not! You might as well agree with who Jesus say you are.

I AM in Jesus and Jesus is in me.
I AM a new creation. Old things are gone and ALL things are being made new!
I AM Jesus' representative to my world.

I AM focused on my Father's business.

I AM God's work of art, created for the work of God.

I AM Ready for ALL the Holy Spirit has for me!
I AM an empowered vessel of the Holy Spirit.
I AM a loved Child of God and He is proud of me!
I AM driven and fed by God's work in my world.

I AM solely empowered by serving like Jesus.

I AM led by God's plan every day!

I AM a vessel of the Holy Spirit's power.

I AM God's agent of reconciliation.

I AM the instigator of Divine Intervention!

I AM empowered to bring healing!

I AM Jesus' fisherman to my world. My joy and peace is the bait and His love is the hook.
I AM empowered to heal and I AM growing in wholeness based on my time alone in God's presence.
I AM the carrier of faith for my world. And if need be, I will carry my friends and tear off roofs!

I AM pure before God so God's power can flow purely through me.

I AM God's bridge into the lives of those I love.

I AM capable of starving my flesh to strengthen my spirit through fasting.

I AM living out of my new thinking and not my old neediness!

I AM a person who invests time in Sabbath life, because that empowers the rest of the time in my life.

I AM healed, filled, and empowered to walk out the life Jesus has poured in!

I AM empowered to be God's answer to life's problems.

I AM blessed because of my Kingdom investment of service.

I AM empowered by my self-sacrifice.

I AM an investor of the life of Jesus.

I AM the carrier of God's will for everyone who I contact.

I AM fruitful in every endeavor of my life!

I AM all Jesus says I am.

This journal is my prophetic title deed and I will see everything written in here.

I am a kingdom seeker, a foot washer.

I lay hands on the sick and they recover.

I cast out demons with a word and they stay out.

I have an anointing that abides.

I am growing in character, growing in power, and hearing God's voice better every day.

I am preparing to do the greater works Jesus promised.

I go into all the world and make disciple-making disciples.

I love fighting the devil, and love enforcing God's will,

I grow stronger as I pray, longer because what God promised he can produce.
I do not grow weary in well doing, I get stronger day by day.
I know God's working for my good because I love him and am seeking his purpose.
I am a co-heir with Jesus, am seated in high places with Jesus.
Greater is the Spirit within me then everything in the world.
No weapon formed against me will succeed and everything that comes against me is accursed.
I am blessed by God and cannot be cursed.
I am crucified with Christ and Christ lives through me.
I am undefeatable because the life of Jesus flows through the wounds of this life.
I am free of hurts and wounds of my past.
I am free of demonic chains.
I am free of bitterness and unforgiveness.
I am on a path that shines fuller like a sunrise.

About the Author

Pastor Sean Lumsden graduated from Azusa Pacific University in 1992 with a Bachelor's Degree in Theology and a Minor in Biblical Greek. These degrees were immediately put to use as Sean started in an 18 year career as a waiter.

In 1996, Sean was licensed as a Pastor from the International Church of the Foursquare Gospel. Shortly after, he planted "jacob's ladder;" one of the first 'Gen-x' churches in the nation. Not a particularly large church, their slogan was "come to jacob's ladder and get alone with God."

Eventually Sean and his family went to Spokane, Washington where Sean helped start a few churches.

Additionally, he worked as a financial planner, national-award winning advertising copywriter, radio disc-jockey, music instructor and again as a waiter.

Currently, Sean is the pastor of Living Hope Foursquare; a funky little church in a funky part of Spokane. At Living Hope, their church aims to make people 'Jesus-ish'. Their slogan is 'creating Christ-like people who love people like Christ.'

On December 27, 2018, Sean's beloved wife of 25 ½ years, Lynne, passed away. The Lilac color of this cover is in honor of her. Lynne's passionate commitment to better the lives of deaf people was an inspiration to everyone she met. She became the top sign-language interpreter in the country while battling mental health issues. Sadly, those issues caught up with her and led to her early death.

Sean still writes commercials while he pastors, and in his spare time he hangs out with his family, collects musical instruments, plays tennis and takes his Saabs into the shop for repairs.

This is the fifth book in the '30 Days on:' series. Sean had amazing sales in 2019 when he sold 4 books, doubling the sales total from the past 5 years.

You can contact Sean at PastorSean@LivingHopeSpokane.com.

Made in the USA
Middletown, DE
29 June 2019